Printed in Great Britain
by Amazon

19421756R00071